MANAGEMENT
THROUGH PUZZLES

By Rani Selvanathan

West Chester University

Bassim Hamadeh, CEO and Publisher
Michael Simpson, Vice President of Acquisitions
Jamie Giganti, Managing Editor
Jess Busch, Graphic Design Supervisor
Melissa Barcomb, Acquisitions Editor
Sarah Wheeler, Senior Project Editor
Stephanie Sandler, Licensing Associate

First published in the United States of America in 2014 by Cognella, Inc.

Printed in the United States of America

ISBN: 978-1-62131-814-9 (pbk)/ 978-1-62131-815-6 (br)

www.cognella.com 800-200-3908

Contents

About the Book and How to Use It

This book is a novel way of retaining and reviewing of management concepts. Management concepts as taught in a classroom or in any other way covers a wide range of topics which become difficult to recall with the passing of time. Reviewing concepts in a relaxed manner, by spending time looking for clues that guide towards the correct answer is surely a means to improve quality of retention. Quality of retention can be defined as the amount of information retained and the time over which the retention takes place.

This work uses crossword puzzles to promote retention and can be used with any standard textbook on Management. The book is divided according to the topic covered in a typical management classroom. Each topic is addressed to by means of a crossword puzzle with clues leading to finding of terms, technology, and application covered in that topic, The later half of the book provides the answer key to the puzzle.

This book can be used with any textbook dealing with the basic principles of management at the graduate or undergraduate level. It can further be used by managers as 1) a productive way to spend time, and 2) to recall a concept that one is distantly familiar with.

About the Author

Dr. Rani Selvanathan is an Associate Professor of Management at West Chester University, Pennsylvania. She has a background in Management Science and in Production and Operations Management. She is also certified by American Production and Inventory Control Society as CPIM.

Introduction to Management

Across

4 One of the four functions of management
6 Unwritten code of conduct
7 Skills needed by top managers
11 Offering goods/services needed by the customer
13 Current-day competition to retail stores (2 words)
16 Also known as first-line managers
18 Group of people getting together for a common purpose
19 One of the drawbacks of bureaucracy

Down

1 Involve participation of more than one country
2 Introduced by Max Weber
3 To keep the level of enthusiasm high
5 Noun signifying a varied background
8 A by product of scientific management (2 words)
9 A drawback of scientific management
10 A top-level manager
12 Offering goods/services by keeping costs down

21 Putting people and work together to reach organization's goals
23 Also known as first-line managers
24 Abbreviation for standard operating procedures

14 Checking to see if our actions have the desired effect
15 Skills needed by lower-level managers
17 Knack of getting along with people (2 words)
20 Father of Scientific Management
22 Written-down do's and don't's in an organization

Organizational Culture

Across

1 A trait of being dedicated to the work on hand

6 Managers' guide to their actions and conduct

7 Locus of control can either be internal or ________

9 Communication of an organizational culture can be done through this

10 Openness to this is likely to make managers innovative and willing to take risks

11 Critical thinking may be the outcome of this mood

Down

2 The opposite of extroverts

3 Trait that makes one critical of self and others all the time (2 words)

4 People high in this feel good about themselves and what they can do (2 words)

5 Are formed by terminal values of the organization

8 This makes a manager go above and beyond the call of duty

12 The ability to get along well with others

14 The culture of an organization is its ________

13 _______ intelligence is the ability of managers to manage their moods as well as those of their subordinates
15 Working towards pre-set goals and awaiting feedback are seen in a person whose orientation is this
18 This increases as people move up in the managerial hierarchical ladder (2 words)
21 Whom does organizational culture begin with?
22 Determine a manager's approach to work
24 New employees learn about organization's values and norms from organizational _______
25 You like controlling and influencing others, your need for _______ is high
16 A short-lived but intense state of mind
17 Value arising out of beliefs on modes of behavior
19 State of mind
20 People who shape organizational culture
23 Satisfied managers are less likely to do this

Ethics and Management

Across

3 Sells the finished product made by a company to customers
4 An invisible barrier in an organization or a society (2 words)
6 ________ ethics is influenced by family and peers
9 That which protects one's fundamental rights (2 words)
11 People or group affected by a company
13 Inner guiding moral principles, values, and beliefs
14 Are considered a very critical stakeholder group

Down

1 A situation where a manager has to choose between a good and a bad decision (2 words)
2 He/she invests money in a company
5 Coordinates efforts and cooperation between individuals
7 An easily explainable action comes under ________ rule
8 Rule that causes the greatest good to a large number of people
10 A role model
12 Rule that distributes benefits and harms equally

16 A tire manufacturing company is a _______ to a car company
17 The esteem gained by an organization that is behaving ethically
19 Differences among people
20 People who work in a company

15 What is considered ethical is usually _______
18 The confidence one has in a company

Globalization

Across

3 One of the forces in the general environment
4 An organization that operates in more than one country
6 Immigration, more women entering the work force are examples of ________ forces
8 Is one of the barriers to entry (2 words)
11 An orientation of a society that values performance, success, results

Down

1 Inflation is one of the ________ forces
2 This could be negatively affected by outsourcing
5 How often managers should monitor the general environment
7 The values of a group is of greater importance than those of an individual
9 Number of forces in the general environment
10 This culture is subject to change over time

13 Set of forces external to the organization that affect its operations
14 ______ environments influence managers on a practically daily basis
19 These hinder new competition from coming up
21 What the search for lowering production costs has led to
22 The doctrine that is one of the causes of outsourcing (2 words)
25 The effect of forces in the task environment (2 words)

12 One of the forces of task environment
15 Individuals and/or groups looking to buy available goods/services
16 Tax imposed by a government on goods imported by a country
17 ______ competition could be a problem in the future
18 Routine social conventions
20 A culturally diverse management is a source of ______ to a company
23 Norms that are central to the functioning of a society
24 Abbreviation for General Agreement on Tariffs and Trade

Decision Making

Across

2 _______ judgment requires careful analysis
5 Response to opportunities or threats
9 The most appropriate decision under the circumstances
10 The process of choosing one alternative from among several (2 words)
12 When members of a group strive for agreement
13 Encouraging this may reduce groupthink
15 Other ways of doing things

Down

1 Probability that a certain outcome will occur
3 That which is acceptable
4 What the classical model of decision making is
6 Can be done through cost-benefit analysis (2 words)
7 These decisions are made in response to an unpredictable situation
8 Information that has multiple interpretations
11 Tells you if your decision is right or wrong

19 Problem _______ is the first step in the decision-making process
21 Contends that decision making is basically risky and uncertain (2 words)
23 Decision made by an office manager to order supplies
24 The gut feeling that makes you decide
25 When you are not sure of the outcome

14 Plays the role of a critic in a decision-making process (2 words)
16 Another reason for incomplete information
17 These lower performances (2 words)
18 Existence of discrepancy between desired and actual state of affairs
20 Programmed decisions are usually this
22 The number of criteria that influence the selection of an alternative

Planning and Strategy

Across

1 A planning horizon that lasts up to one year (2 words)

6 Combined performance is greater than the sum of the individual ones

9 Happens when a company becomes its own supplier (2 words)

10 Decisions concerning an organization's mission and goals (2 words)

Down

2 Results in benefits from synergy (2 words)

3 A state of permanent, ongoing, and intense competition

4 Loss of customer goodwill could be a _______ for an organization

5 At this level of planning, how to compete in a given market is decided

11 A plan that could be used for a non-programmed decision (2 words)
14 The purpose of an organization (2 words)
15 A strategy where products are customized to suit national conditions
19 Done by managers responsible for increasing efficiency and effectiveness (2 words)
20 What is needed to prepare a plan
22 Setting goals for the future
23 Strategy of General Electric in acquiring NBC
24 A strategy to attract customers by reducing the cost of operations (2 words)
25 What forecasts always are

6 An analysis where your opportunities and threats are examined
7 Its level affects the profit an organization could make
8 A strategy of making your product different and distinct from the other
12 When a business makes its position in its current industry stronger
13 What organizations do when selling their products in another country
16 The intended duration of a plan (2 words)
17 A plan that is used repeatedly (2 words)
18 Set of decisions made to reach a goal
21 Strategy intended for a market segment

Organizing

Across

5 ________ of authority specifies the relative authority a manager has
6 This kind of structure can satisfy the needs of diverse customers
10 Perceived boundaries between departments are erased when using this (3 words)

Down

1 A system of job and task relationships (2 words)
2 Group of people working together to achieve a common goal
3 He/she plays only an advisory role (2 words)

12 Becomes important when the number of functions and divisions increase
14 When lower-level managers are given the authority to make important decisions
15 Jobs that are this may become boring and monotonous
17 Power vested in a manager to help in making decisions
19 This type of organization has many levels of authority
20 Is a frequent problem with an organization having many levels of authority
24 What a chain of command should be
27 Task _______ measures how meaningful a job is
28 In a product structure, managers _______ in only one product area
29 Process to create a new or change an existing organizational structure
30 _______ structure makes decision-making faster

4 The function that specializes in watching/reacting to new market developments
7 When divisions are organized according to goods/service produced (2 words)
8 Gives rise to "two boss" situation (2 words)
9 Number of factors affecting organizational structure
11 Is the number of subordinates who report to a manager (3 words)
13 _______ structure is suited for a highly skilled workforce
16 Encouraging workers to develop new skills is job
18 One of the factors determining how motivating a job is
21 Outcome when a problem is viewed from a narrow, departmental perspective
22 It is beneficial to have a _______ chain of command
23 A company expanding both home and abroad has this type of structure
25 Another name for an ad hoc committee (2 words)
26 The role played by a manager to increase coordination

Changes in an Organization

Across

1 This measure could overcome the fear of acquiring new technology
4 A change should make an organization more ________
6 Metaphor that illustrates that the need for a change is unpredictable (3 words)
8 When not given sufficient support, these tend to leave the organization to start one of their own
12 The need to make the change comes from customer demand, which is an ________ (2 words)

Down

2 A bottom-up change is likely to reduce this
3 Making the change permanent
4 These people take advantage of new opportunities
5 This idea comes from upper-level management (2 words)
7 When performance is compared with that of the competition (2 words)
9 The function of management that signals a need for change
10 Process signifying a breaking away from status quo

15 A change-agent who helps in the change process
16 Doing something different from a status quo
17 Faced with the need to make a change, organizations have to be this

11 Problem ________s the most important step in the change process
13 This describes the employee reluctance to a change process
14 It is easy to change organizations with these cultures

Motivation

Across

1 Removes factors that encourage dysfunctional behavior
4 _______ goals are less motivational
5 Time, effort, knowledge, skills are characterized as a person's -----
6 What one learns from watching others (2 words)
10 When driven by this, your motivation depends on your desire to control others
11 These could motivate as well

Down

1 What an underpayment inequity could lead to (2 words)
2 Satisfaction of these do not necessarily motivate (2 words)
3 Motivation comes from within
5 Second step in the Expectancy Theory
7 A necessity
8 What motivation is per Equity Theory
9 The lowest level of needs
12 Specific goals are usually this
15 A _______ need is not motivating

13 What a person gets/expects to get as a result of job completion
14 Behavior that is detrimental to the performance of the organization
17 You are comparing your output to that of a _______
22 Lack of fairness
24 The number of levels in Maslow's pyramid
25 This must be high for motivation to be high
26 The desirability of an outcome
27 _______ behavior describes the desire to help others
28 The proponent of "Hierarchy of Needs"

16 A change in employee behavior
18 When motivation comes from an outside source
19 According to Herzberg, _______ are related to work being done
20 This reinforcement is removed when satisfactory work performance is noted
21 When pay is related to performance (2 words)
23 The need to be respected by others

Leaders/Leadership

Across

1 Managers influence their subordinates to reach their goals through this
5 They are not necessarily leaders
8 Leadership is sometimes this
12 States that effectiveness of a leader depends upon the situation (2 words)
14 Leaders are considered this when they express concern for their subordinates

Down

2 What the relationship between leader traits and leader effectiveness is not
3 Have the desire to work for the benefits of others (2 words)
4 Leadership style is sure to depend on these
6 An early approach to leadership (2 words)
7 Because of empowerment, managers may spend less time doing this

15 The power a boss has to assign job duties to the employees
18 Effectiveness of a leader depends on how large this is (2 words)
21 A manager is one if he/she inspires, motivates, provides direction to an employee
22 The driving force of an effective leadership
23 Short-term profit orientation leads to short-term _______
24 Leaders have this structure when they want to make sure that a job is done
25 Leadership styles are _______

9 Sharing of authority with subordinates
10 You may become a role model with this (2 words)
11 Special knowledge and training gives you this (2 words)
13 A behavior that shows managers' concern for subordinates
16 Empowerment usually increases worker _______
17 The means used to motivate and inspire others
19 A way to appreciate a job well done
20 Excessive use of this power limits performance

Team Management

Across

6 Members of this team rarely meet face to face
8 In this stage, members try to get to know one another
9 What a dispersion of the group is known as
11 One of the problems faced by a larger group
13 Another name for departments (2 words)
17 Refers to the number of members in a group (2 words)

Down

1 Splitting the work (3 words)
2 There are ________ stages of group development
3 More organizations are opening up to this
4 Members of a mountaineering club form this (2 words)
5 The technology that enables team members to interact in real time
7 A deviant behavior can sometimes be for the good

21 Members of this have a common concern (2 words)
23 Failure to conform to accepted standards
24 What an ad hoc committee is (2 words)
26 We are more ______ to customers as a result of working in groups

10 Behaviors and tasks a group member must follow (2 words)
11 To be effective, group members should have these skills
12 What managers create to achieve organizational goals (2 words)
14 A group achieves its purpose at this stage
15 These can be large or small
16 Self-managed work groups should be given enough of this
18 Members of a smaller group have limited use of these
19 Groups/teams also increase this
20 ______ groups often provide the social support
22 What one gets when departments or people coordinate their activities
25 A group is not necessarily this

Human Resource Management

Across

1 Group of current employees of an organization
5 The number of major components of human resource management
7 Development of a candidate pool for open positions

Down

2 A strategy that benefits from flexibility and cost
3 This must be preceded by training and development (2 words)
4 This is an important resource for a manager

8 The reason that a structured interview is better than an unstructured one (2 words)
11 Lists what is needed to perform the job (2 words)
13 They represent employee interest in an organization
18 Employees acquire knowledge and skills in this way (2 words)
20 These might represent employee interests (2 words)
23 Open houses and career fairs are means of doing this (2 words)
25 That there is an _______ between trait and performance is questionable
26 This becomes essential after the recruitment

6 Recruitment is this when managers look into existing employees
9 A division or Department of Justice
10 Negotiation between managers and labor unions (2 words)
12 Where work to be completed is sent to other countries
14 Personality tests can be "faked" and hence are _______
15 These tell us the qualifications and the number of people needed in the future (2 words)
16 The ideal frequency of on-the-job-training
17 These should provide the feedback to managers and subordinates alike
19 This is a necessity for managers at all levels
21 What the components of HRM should be
22 An experienced member of the organization who provides guidance
24 Employee performance is better with _______ work experience

Controlling

Across

1 Shared set of beliefs that determines the behavior of workers (2 words)

4 Excess inventory is an indication of an ______ organization

7 Goals are necessary for ______ member of an organization

9 Monitors customer reaction to goods/services (2 words)

12 Measures the organization's ability to meet short-term obligations (2 words)

Down

2 Has the potential to deliver accurate and timely information in an organization (2 words)

3 A good goal should be this

5 Strategy to anticipate problems (3 words)

6 The number of steps in the control process

8 Yet another way to control

10 An organization that uses more debt than equity is highly ______

14 Behavior that is influenced by people around you
17 Useful when activities are routine (2 words)
20 They are developed to determine the allocation of resources (2 words)
22 Abbreviation of a frequently used measure to gauge financial performance
24 A control that gives immediate feedback
25 Direct supervision can do this to the employees

11 All control systems should be this
13 Another way to motivate employees (2 words)
15 What is a difficult but attainable goal (2 words)
16 An organization is rendered this with overuse of bureaucratic control
18 Not just reacting to things after they happen
19 Acronym for Management by Objectives
21 Controlling is ______ to any organization
23 One of the drawbacks of direct supervision

Communication

Across

2 What is lacking in face-to-face communication (2 words)
4 Information is needed to assure this function of management
6 The last phase of the communication process
10 This requires effective communication
13 The one who initiates the feedback phase

Down

1 Transforming messages into understandable language
3 Method(s) to manage information (2 words)
5 Amount of varied information a medium can carry (2 words)
7 What ineffective communication could be
8 Managers need information to make these (2 words)

16 These are on the rise with the growing use of IT in communication

17 What information may go through while being communicated

19 Is only the means used in the communication process

21 DSS only ______ the managers in their tasks

22 A key means of sharing information

23 Too much information causes this (2 words)

25 Raw facts that have neither been summarized nor analyzed

26 The most advanced management information system available (2 words)

27 Is disruptive in any stage of the communication process

28 The kind of information that is meaningful

9 Real-time information takes ______ conditions into account

11 This kind of communication can be used to reinforce verbal communication

12 The one who wants to share some information

14 Advances in Information Technology makes the product life cycle ______

15 Quality information should be this

18 The first phase in the communication process

20 Data when organized and meaningful become this

24 Another characteristic of the quality of information

Operations Management

Across

1 Dramatic change in design to get significant improvement

5 Storage and shortage costs move in this direction

11 The time taken for the order to arrive from the time it was placed (2 words)

12 A possible machine-worker interface (2 words)

14 Managers must make sure that their products have _______ that customers desire

Down

2 Action taken to meet customer demands

3 Quality of a product should be this for the same price

4 This in a product layout could hurt efficiency

6 Here, workstations are relatively self-contained (2 words)

7 This comes down as the level of items in stock increases

8 The father of organizational quality assurance (2 words)

16 Gross revenue divided by the total costs of operation
17 Signals the need to place an order again (2 words)
20 We are left with this when we make more than we can sell
22 Time needed to set up equipment is usually this
23 These costs are also known as inventory costs
24 This is how workers are in a product layout
25 A good quality product should be this
26 The total cost of carrying inventory is this when storage and shortage costs are equal

9 Buffer stock improves this (2 words)
10 Total costs of carrying inventory is a sum of storage costs and this (2 words)
13 Another name for mass production (2 words)
15 A quality assurance concept (2 words)
18 The name of the system that changes raw materials to finished goods
19 To have a higher productivity, the associated costs must do this
21 An organization is without a _______ stock when using just-in-time inventory

1 SOLUTION
2 PUZZLES
3 TO

Introduction to Management

Across

4 One of the four functions of management
6 Unwritten code of conduct
7 Skills needed by top managers
11 Offering goods/services needed by the customer
13 Current-day competition to retail stores (2 words)
16 Also known as first-line managers
18 Group of people getting together for a common purpose
19 One of the drawbacks of bureaucracy

Down

1 Involve participation of more than one country
2 Introduced by Max Weber
3 To keep the level of enthusiasm high
5 Noun signifying a varied background
8 A by product of scientific management (2 words)
9 A drawback of scientific management
10 A top-level manager
12 Offering goods/services by keeping costs down

21 Putting people and work together to reach organization's goals
23 Also known as first-line managers
24 Abbreviation for standard operating procedures

14 Checking to see if our actions have the desired effect
15 Skills needed by lower-level managers
17 Knack of getting along with people (2 words)
20 Father of Scientific Management
22 Written-down do's and don't's in an organization

Organizational Culture

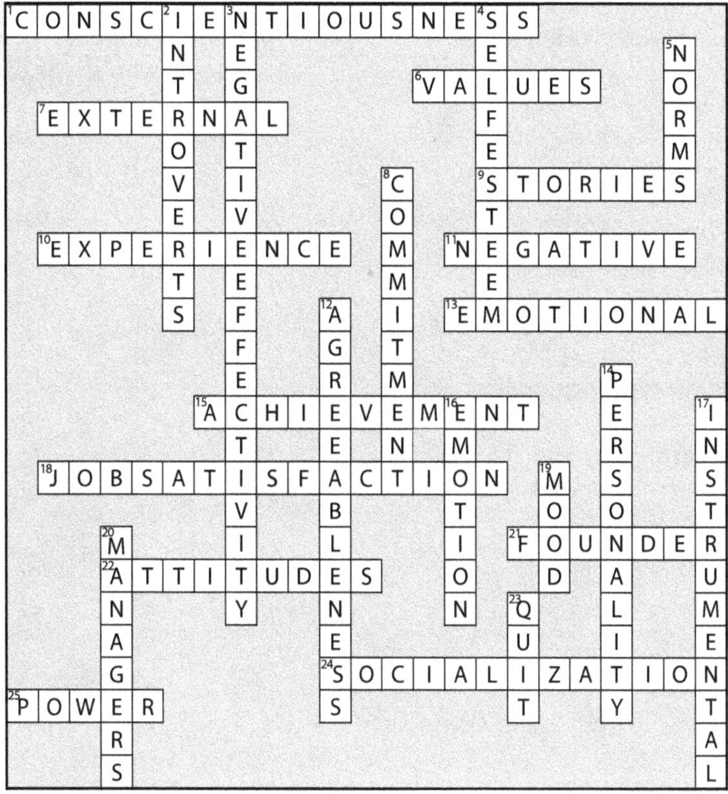

Across

1 A trait of being dedicated to the work on hand

6 Managers' guide to their actions and conduct

7 Locus of control can either be internal or ________

9 Communication of an organizational culture can be done through this

10 Openness to this is likely to make managers innovative and willing to take risks

11 Critical thinking may be the outcome of this mood

Down

2 The opposite of extroverts

3 Trait that makes one critical of self and others all the time (2 words)

4 People high in this feel good about themselves and what they can do (2 words)

5 Are formed by terminal values of the organization

8 This makes a manager go above and beyond the call of duty

12 The ability to get along well with others

13 ______ intelligence is the ability of managers to manage their moods as well as those of their subordinates
15 Working towards pre-set goals and awaiting feedback are seen in a person whose orientation is this
18 This increases as people move up in the managerial hierarchical ladder (2 words)
21 Whom does organizational culture begin with?
22 Determine a manager's approach to work
24 New employees learn about organization's values and norms from organizational ______
25 You like controlling and influencing others, your need for ______ is high
14 The culture of an organization is its ______
16 A short-lived but intense state of mind
17 Value arising out of beliefs on modes of behavior
19 State of mind
20 People who shape organizational culture
23 Satisfied managers are less likely to do this

Ethics and Management

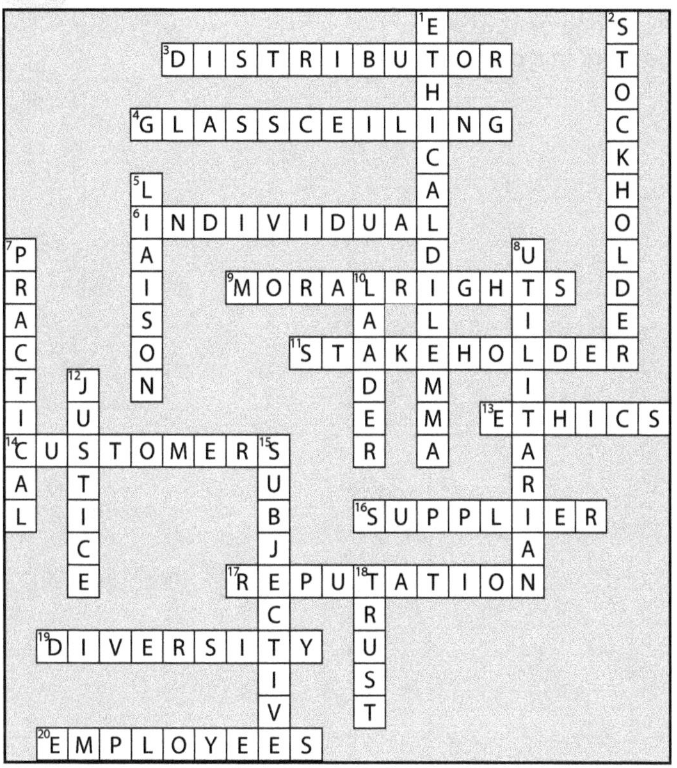

Across

3 Sells the finished product made by a company to customers

4 An invisible barrier in an organization or a society (2 words)

6 _______ ethics is influenced by family and peers

9 That which protects one's fundamental rights (2 words)

11 People or group affected by a company

13 Inner guiding moral principles, values, and beliefs

14 Are considered a very critical stakeholder group

Down

1 A situation where a manager has to choose between a good and a bad decision (2 words)

2 He/she invests money in a company

5 Coordinates efforts and cooperation between individuals

7 An easily explainable action comes under _______ rule

8 Rule that causes the greatest good to a large number of people

10 A role model

12 Rule that distributes benefits and harms equally

16 A tire manufacturing company is a _______ to a car company
17 The esteem gained by an organization that is behaving ethically
19 Differences among people
20 People who work in a company

15 What is considered ethical is usually _______
18 The confidence one has in a company

Globalization

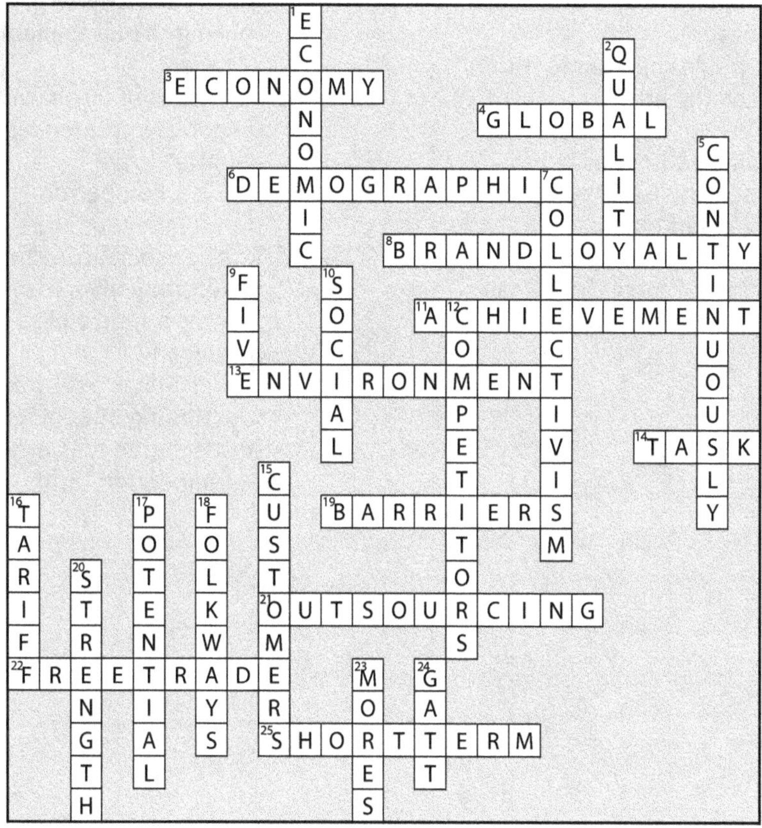

Across

3 One of the forces in the general environment
4 An organization that operates in more than one country
6 Immigration, more women entering the work force are examples of _______ forces
8 Is one of the barriers to entry (2 words)
11 An orientation of a society that values performance, success, results

Down

1 Inflation is one of the _______ forces
2 This could be negatively affected by outsourcing
5 How often managers should monitor the general environment
7 The values of a group is of greater importance than those of an individual
9 Number of forces in the general environment

13 Set of forces external to the organization that affect its operations
14 _______ environments influence managers on a practically daily basis
19 These hinder new competition from coming up
21 What the search for lowering production costs has led to
22 The doctrine that is one of the causes of outsourcing (2 words)
25 The effect of forces in the task environment (2 words)

10 This culture is subject to change over time
12 One of the forces of task environment
15 Individuals and/or groups looking to buy available goods/ services
16 Tax imposed by a government on goods imported by a country
17 _______ competition could be a problem in the future
18 Routine social conventions
20 A culturally diverse management is a source of _______ to a company
23 Norms that are central to the functioning of a society
24 Abbreviation for General Agreement on Tariffs and Trade

Decision Making

										[1]R				[2]R	E	A	[3]S	O	N	E	D		
	[4]P				[5]D	[6]E	C	I	S	I	O	[7]N	S				A						[8]A
	R					C				S		O			[9]O	P	T	I	M	U	M		M
[10]D	E	C	I	S	I	O	N	M	A	K	I	N	G				I						B
	S					N						P					S						I
	C		[11]F			O						R					F						G
	R		E			M				[12]G	R	O	U	P	T	H	I	N	K				U
[13]D	I	V	E	R	S	I	T	Y				G					C						O
	P		D			C						R			[14]D		I						U
	T		B			F						[15]A	L	T	E	R	N	A	[16]T	I	V	E	S
	I		A			E						M			V		G		I				
	V		C			A		[17]B				M			I				M				
	E		K			S		A				E			L				E				
						I		D				D			’						[18]P		
						B		D							S						R		
						[19]I	D	E	N	T	I	F	I	C	A	T	I	O	N		O		
						L		C							D						B		
[20]R			[21]A	D	M	I	N	I	S	T	R	A	T	I	V	E	M	O	D	E	L		
O						T		S							O						E		
U			[22]F			Y		I							C						M		
T			O					O		[23]P	R	O	G	R	A	M	M	E	D				
[24]I	N	T	U	I	T	I	O	N							T								
N			R					S				[25]U	N	C	E	R	T	A	I	N			
E																							

Across

2 _______ judgment requires careful analysis

5 Response to opportunities or threats

9 The most appropriate decision under the circumstances

10 The process of choosing one alternative from among several (2 words)

12 When members of a group strive for agreement

13 Encouraging this may reduce groupthink

15 Other ways of doing things

Down

1 Probability that a certain outcome will occur

3 That which is acceptable

4 What the classical model of decision making is

6 Can be done through cost-benefit analysis (2 words)

7 These decisions are made in response to an unpredictable situation

8 Information that has multiple interpretations

11 Tells you if your decision is right or wrong

19 Problem ______ is the first step in the decision-making process
21 Contends that decision making is basically risky and uncertain (2 words)
23 Decision made by an office manager to order supplies
24 The gut feeling that makes you decide
25 When you are not sure of the outcome
14 Plays the role of a critic in a decision-making process (2 words)
16 Another reason for incomplete information
17 These lower performances (2 words)
18 Existence of discrepancy between desired and actual state of affairs
20 Programmed decisions are usually this
22 The number of criteria that influence the selection of an alternative

Planning and Strategy

Across

1 A planning horizon that lasts up to one year (2 words)

6 Combined performance is greater than the sum of the individual ones

9 Happens when a company becomes its own supplier (2 words)

10 Decisions concerning an organization's mission and goals (2 words)

Down

2 Results in benefits from synergy (2 words)

3 A state of permanent, ongoing, and intense competition

4 Loss of customer goodwill could be a _______ for an organization

5 At this level of planning, how to compete in a given market is decided

11 A plan that could be used for a non-programmed decision (2 words)
14 The purpose of an organization (2 words)
15 A strategy where products are customized to suit national conditions
19 Done by managers responsible for increasing efficiency and effectiveness (2 words)
20 What is needed to prepare a plan
22 Setting goals for the future
23 Strategy of General Electric in acquiring NBC
24 A strategy to attract customers by reducing the cost of operations (2 words)
25 What forecasts always are

6 An analysis where your opportunities and threats are examined
7 Its level affects the profit an organization could make
8 A strategy of making your product different and distinct from the other
12 When a business makes its position in its current industry stronger
13 What organizations do when selling their products in another country
16 The intended duration of a plan (2 words)
17 A plan that is used repeatedly (2 words)
18 Set of decisions made to reach a goal
21 Strategy intended for a market segment

Organizing

Across

5 _______ of authority specifies the relative authority a manager has

6 This kind of structure can satisfy the needs of diverse customers

10 Perceived boundaries between departments are erased when using this (3 words)

Down

1 A system of job and task relationships (2 words)

2 Group of people working together to achieve a common goal

3 He/she plays only an advisory role (2 words)

12 Becomes important when the number of functions and divisions increase
14 When lower-level managers are given the authority to make important decisions
15 Jobs that are this may become boring and monotonous
17 Power vested in a manager to help in making decisions
19 This type of organization has many levels of authority
20 Is a frequent problem with an organization having many levels of authority
24 What a chain of command should be
27 Task _______ measures how meaningful a job is
28 In a product structure, managers _______ in only one product area
29 Process to create a new or change an existing organizational structure
30 _______ structure makes decision-making faster

4 The function that specializes in watching/reacting to new market developments
7 When divisions are organized according to goods/service produced (2 words)
8 Gives rise to "two boss" situation (2 words)
9 Number of factors affecting organizational structure
11 Is the number of subordinates who report to a manager (3 words)
13 _______ structure is suited for a highly skilled workforce
16 Encouraging workers to develop new skills is job
18 One of the factors determining how motivating a job is
21 Outcome when a problem is viewed from a narrow, departmental perspective
22 It is beneficial to have a _______ chain of command
23 A company expanding both home and abroad has this type of structure
25 Another name for an ad hoc committee (2 words)
26 The role played by a manager to increase coordination

Changes in an Organization

1 T	2 R	A	I	N	I	N	G							3 R					
	E										4 E	F	F	E	C	5 T	I	V	E
	S										N			F		O			
	I			6 W	H	I	T	E	W	A	T	E	R	R	A	P	I	D	S
	S										R			E		D			
	T										E			E		O			
	A						7 B				P			Z		W			
8 I	N	T	R	A	P	R	E	N	E	U	R	S		I		N			
	C						N				E			N					
	E		C				C				N			G					
			O				H		10 U		E								
			N				M		N		U		11 R						
	12 E	X	T	E	13 R	N	A	L	F	O	R	C	E		14 F				
			R		E		R		R		S		C		L				
			O		S		K		E				O		E				
			L		I		I		E				G		X				
			L		S		N		Z				N		I				
			I		T		G		I				I		B				
			N		A				N		15 C	A	T	A	L	Y	S	T	
			G		N				G				I		E				
					C								O						
16 C	H	A	N	G	E			17 R	E	S	P	O	N	S	I	V	E		

Across

1 This measure could overcome the fear of acquiring new technology

4 A change should make an organization more ________

6 Metaphor that illustrates that the need for a change is unpredictable (3 words)

8 When not given sufficient support, these tend to leave the organization to start one of their own

12 The need to make the change comes from customer demand, which is an ________ (2 words)

Down

2 A bottom-up change is likely to reduce this

3 Making the change permanent

4 These people take advantage of new opportunities

5 This idea comes from upper-level management (2 words)

7 When performance is compared with that of the competition (2 words)

9 The function of management that signals a need for change

10 Process signifying a breaking away from status quo

15 A change-agent who helps in the change process
16 Doing something different from a status quo
17 Faced with the need to make a change, organizations have to be this

11 Problem ______s the most important step in the change process
13 This describes the employee reluctance to a change process
14 It is easy to change organizations with these cultures

Motivation

Across

1 Removes factors that encourage dysfunctional behavior
4 _______ goals are less motivational
5 Time, effort, knowledge, skills are characterized as a person's -----
6 What one learns from watching others (2 words)
10 When driven by this, your motivation depends on your desire to control others
11 These could motivate as well

Down

1 What an underpayment inequity could lead to (2 words)
2 Satisfaction of these do not necessarily motivate (2 words)
3 Motivation comes from within
5 Second step in the Expectancy Theory
7 A necessity
8 What motivation is per Equity Theory
9 The lowest level of needs
12 Specific goals are usually this
15 A _______ need is not motivating

13 What a person gets/expects to get as a result of job completion
14 Behavior that is detrimental to the performance of the organization
17 You are comparing your output to that of a _______
22 Lack of fairness
24 The number of levels in Maslow's pyramid
25 This must be high for motivation to be high
26 The desirability of an outcome
27 _______ behavior describes the desire to help others
28 The proponent of "Hierarchy of Needs"
16 A change in employee behavior
18 When motivation comes from an outside source
19 According to Herzberg, _______ are related to work being done
20 This reinforcement is removed when satisfactory work performance is noted
21 When pay is related to performance (2 words)
23 The need to be respected by others

Leaders/Leadership

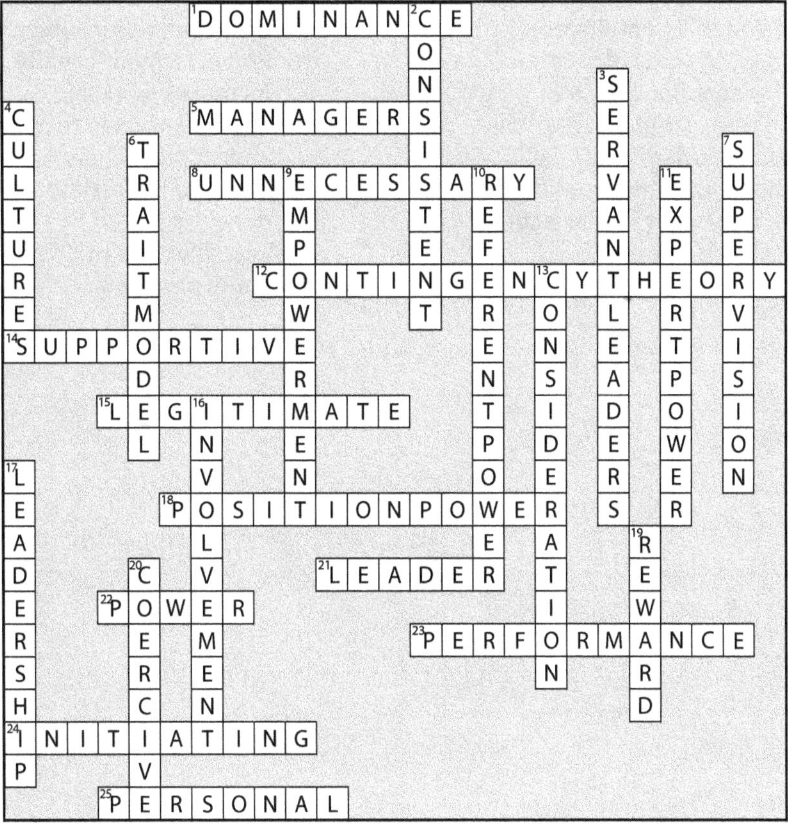

Across

1 Managers influence their subordinates to reach their goals through this
5 They are not necessarily leaders
8 Leadership is sometimes this
12 States that effectiveness of a leader depends upon the situation (2 words)
14 Leaders are considered this when they express concern for their subordinates
15 The power a boss has to assign job duties to the employees

Down

2 What the relationship between leader traits and leader effectiveness is not
3 Have the desire to work for the benefits of others (2 words)
4 Leadership style is sure to depend on these
6 An early approach to leadership (2 words)
7 Because of empowerment, managers may spend less time doing this
9 Sharing of authority with subordinates

18 Effectiveness of a leader depends on how large this is (2 words)
21 A manager is one if he/she inspires, motivates, provides direction to an employee
22 The driving force of an effective leadership
23 Short-term profit orientation leads to short-term _______
24 Leaders have this structure when they want to make sure that a job is done
25 Leadership styles are _______

10 You may become a role model with this (2 words)
11 Special knowledge and training gives you this (2 words)
13 A behavior that shows managers' concern for subordinates
16 Empowerment usually increases worker _______
17 The means used to motivate and inspire others
19 A way to appreciate a job well done
20 Excessive use of this power limits performance

Team Management

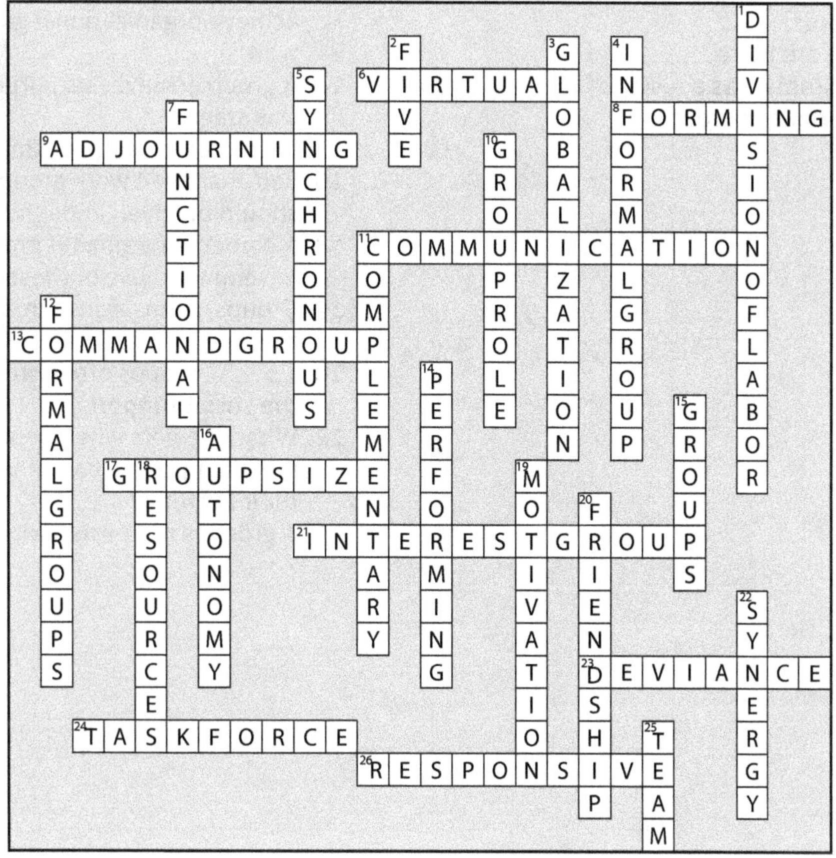

Across

6 Members of this team rarely meet face to face
8 In this stage, members try to get to know one another
9 What a dispersion of the group is known as
11 One of the problems faced by a larger group
13 Another name for departments (2 words)
17 Refers to the number of members in a group (2 words)

Down

1 Splitting the work (3 words)
2 There are ________ stages of group development
3 More organizations are opening up to this
4 Members of a mountaineering club form this (2 words)
5 The technology that enables team members to interact in real time
7 A deviant behavior can sometimes be for the good

21 Members of this have a common concern (2 words)
23 Failure to conform to accepted standards
24 What an ad hoc committee is (2 words)
26 We are more _______ to customers as a result of working in groups

10 Behaviors and tasks a group member must follow (2 words)
11 To be effective, group members should have these skills
12 What managers create to achieve organizational goals (2 words)
14 A group achieves its purpose at this stage
15 These can be large or small
16 Self-managed work groups should be given enough of this
18 Members of a smaller group have limited use of these
19 Groups/teams also increase this
20 _______ groups often provide the social support
22 What one gets when departments or people coordinate their activities
25 A group is not necessarily this

Human Resource Management

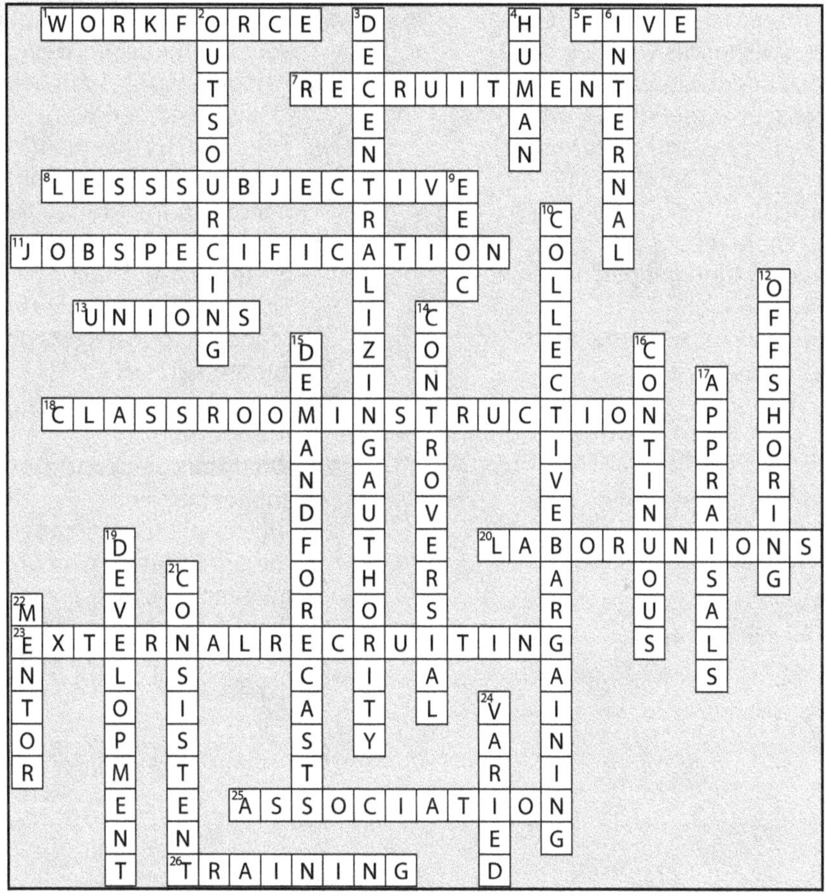

Across

1 Group of current employees of an organization
5 The number of major components of human resource management
7 Development of a candidate pool for open positions

Down

2 A strategy that benefits from flexibility and cost
3 This must be preceded by training and development (2 words)
4 This is an important resource for a manager

8 The reason that a structured interview is better than an unstructured one (2 words)
11 Lists what is needed to perform the job (2 words)
13 They represent employee interest in an organization
18 Employees acquire knowledge and skills in this way (2 words)
20 These might represent employee interests (2 words)
23 Open houses and career fairs are means of doing this (2 words)
25 That there is an ______ between trait and performance is questionable
26 This becomes essential after the recruitment

6 Recruitment is this when managers look into existing employees
9 A division or Department of Justice
10 Negotiation between managers and labor unions (2 words)
12 Where work to be completed is sent to other countries
14 Personality tests can be "faked" and hence are ______
15 These tell us the qualifications and the number of people needed in the future (2 words)
16 The ideal frequency of on-the-job-training
17 These should provide the feedback to managers and subordinates alike
19 This is a necessity for managers at all levels
21 What the components of HRM should be
22 An experienced member of the organization who provides guidance
24 Employee performance is better with ______ work experience

Controlling

Across

1 Shared set of beliefs that determines the behavior of workers (2 words)

4 Excess inventory is an indication of an ______ organization

7 Goals are necessary for ______ member of an organization

9 Monitors customer reaction to goods/services (2 words)

Down

2 Has the potential to deliver accurate and timely information in an organization (2 words)

3 A good goal should be this

5 Strategy to anticipate problems (3 words)

6 The number of steps in the control process

8 Yet another way to control

12 Measures the organization's ability to meet short-term obligations (2 words)
14 Behavior that is influenced by people around you
17 Useful when activities are routine (2 words)
20 They are developed to determine the allocation of resources (2 words)
22 Abbreviation of a frequently used measure to gauge financial performance
24 A control that gives immediate feedback
25 Direct supervision can do this to the employees

10 An organization that uses more debt than equity is highly ______
11 All control systems should be this
13 Another way to motivate employees (2 words)
15 What is a difficult but attainable goal (2 words)
16 An organization is rendered this with overuse of bureaucratic control
18 Not just reacting to things after they happen
19 Acronym for Management by Objectives
21 Controlling is ______ to any organization
23 One of the drawbacks of direct supervision

Communication

Across

2 What is lacking in face-to-face communication (2 words)
4 Information is needed to assure this function of management
6 The last phase of the communication process
10 This requires effective communication
13 The one who initiates the feedback phase

Down

1 Transforming messages into understandable language
3 Method(s) to manage information (2 words)
5 Amount of varied information a medium can carry (2 words)
7 What ineffective communication could be
8 Managers need information to make these (2 words)

16 These are on the rise with the growing use of IT in communication
17 What information may go through while being communicated
19 Is only the means used in the communication process
21 DSS only ______ the managers in their tasks
22 A key means of sharing information
23 Too much information causes this (2 words)
25 Raw facts that have neither been summarized nor analyzed
26 The most advanced management information system available (2 words)
27 Is disruptive in any stage of the communication process
28 The kind of information that is meaningful

9 Real-time information takes ______ conditions into account
11 This kind of communication can be used to reinforce verbal communication
12 The one who wants to share some information
14 Advances in Information Technology makes the product life cycle ______
15 Quality information should be this
18 The first phase in the communication process
20 Data when organized and meaningful become this
24 Another characteristic of the quality of information

Operations Management

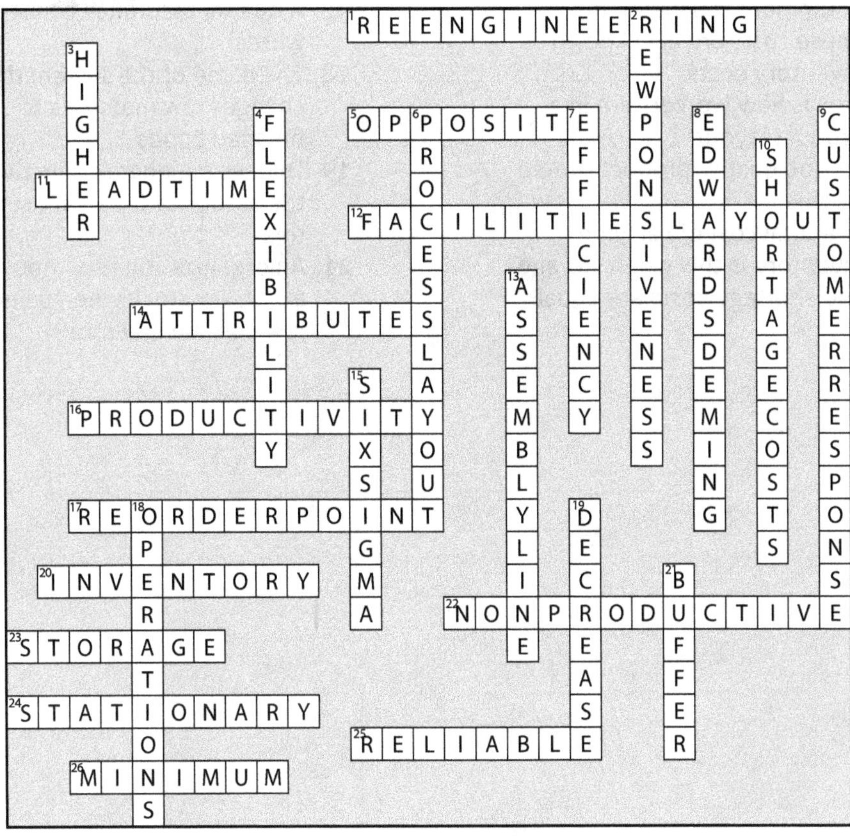

Across

1 Dramatic change in design to get significant improvement
5 Storage and shortage costs move in this direction
11 The time taken for the order to arrive from the time it was placed (2 words)
12 A possible machine-worker interface (2 words)
14 Managers must make sure that their products have ______ that customers desire
16 Gross revenue divided by the total costs of operation

Down

2 Action taken to meet customer demands
3 Quality of a product should be this for the same price
4 This in a product layout could hurt efficiency
6 Here, workstations are relatively self-contained (2 words)
7 This comes down as the level of items in stock increases
8 The father of organizational quality assurance (2 words)
9 Buffer stock improves this (2 words)

17 Signals the need to place an order again (2 words)
20 We are left with this when we make more than we can sell
22 Time needed to set up equipment is usually this
23 These costs are also known as inventory costs
24 This is how workers are in a product layout
25 A good quality product should be this
26 The total cost of carrying inventory is this when storage and shortage costs are equal
10 Total costs of carrying inventory is a sum of storage costs and this (2 words)
13 Another name for mass production (2 words)
15 A quality assurance concept (2 words)
18 The name of the system that changes raw materials to finished goods
19 To have a higher productivity, the associated costs must do this
21 An organization is without a _______ stock when using just-in-time inventory

www.ingramcontent.com/pod-product-compliance
Lightning Source LLC
Chambersburg PA
CBHW081437270326
41932CB00019B/3236

* 9 7 8 1 6 2 1 3 1 8 1 4 9 *